Croydon from Above

GW00778577

Photographs from the period 1870 – 1999

**Front Cover – Katharine Street –
9th September 1999**
Viewed from the tower of the Town Hall on a sunny September afternoon, the 1960s architecture on the left contrasts with the ornate Victorian roof line of the 1896 building with its rows of chimney pots. If recently announced proposals for the massive Park Place redevelopment come to fruition, Ellis House on the left will be demolished but St. George's House, extreme left, will remain.

**Back Cover – Town Centre Looking South –
1st September 1999**
This dramatic view looking down on Wellesley Road and Park Lane clearly illustrates the sudden change from the commercial to residential districts. The railway line south from East Croydon with Park Hill are towards top left and the Whitgift Centre is bottom right. The Tramlink track can be seen in Wellesley Road (bottom centre).

Frontispiece – Town Centre Looking North East – 1st September 1999
Park Lane and St George's House are bottom centre, with East Croydon Station towards centre right. The new tram tracks can be seen in George Street. Cherry Orchard and Oval Roads are towards top centre.

£6.75

Contents

Edited by **John Gent and Tom Samson**

**Published by CNHSS - Croydon Natural History and
Scientific Society**
96a Brighton Road
South Croydon
Surrey CR2 6AD

ISBN 0 906047 13 7

Printed by Design & Print (Sussex) Ltd

64 pages   101 illustrations

1

Introduction

This is the seventh illustrated book published by the Croydon Natural History and Scientific Society during the past 30 years. When the first, *Croydon, the story of a hundred years*, was published to celebrate the society's centenary there were no other local history books in print dealing with Croydon's past. Many more have appeared in recent years but none has taken a look at the town from unusual viewpoints.

Croydon from Above has therefore been compiled to show aspects of the town that few people will have seen before. Some, particularly the earlier views, were taken from high buildings such as the towers of the Parish Church and the Town Hall, one dating from around 1870. Most, however are aerial views and the town has been particularly fortunate that as the home of London's airport in the 1920s and 1930s, a large number of contemporary aerial pictures survive showing parts of the area as urban development was taking place. In later years Handford Photography (now Chorley Handford), based locally, has been a leading company in the field of aerial photography, with a national reputation. Under the guidance of

Tom Samson, joint editor of this publication, Handford's compiled an archive of many hundreds of photographs recording the redevelopment of Croydon and especially the town centre from the late 1950s. Paul Proctor undertakes the company's present aerial photography and has helped greatly by providing examples of his recent work specially taken for inclusion in this book. A brief history of Handford Photography is on page 36 and nearly all the photographs from that page onwards were taken by the company.

In selecting the illustrations we have tried to cover most parts of the present borough. The quality of some of the earlier views is not as good as the later ones because many have been copied and enlarged from postcards issued by Surrey Flying Services in the 1920s or from photographs held in the Local Studies Library.

Croydon from Above provides a unique record of our town and its surroundings as it has developed during the past 100 years. It is to be hoped a similar record will be available for the 21st Century.

1 John Gent
John has many interests and has edited or written ten books, mainly on the Croydon area. He is co-editor, with Tom Samson, of this one. Born in Croydon, he has always lived in the area and since the age of about 15 has been interested in the history of the town. He joined the Croydon Natural History and Scientific Society in 1959, has been a member of its Council for 35 years, and has been President three times. He was Founder Chairman of the Croydon Society and is a Vice-President. Many of the illustrations in the following pages are from his extensive collection.

2 Croydon from an Aeroplane about 1924
This enlargement from a postcard view shows
an Avro 504 of Surrey Flying Services over
the town centre. The Town Hall, Katharine
Street and Park Lane are in the foreground.

Views from Parish Church Tower Looking North East

3 About 1870 – *above*
4 About 1910 – *below*
5 About 1938 – *opposite above*
6 6th September 1999 – *opposite below*

These four photographs provide a fascinating comparison of the view from the same vantage point over a period of 130 years. Tamworth Road is to the left and Reeves Corner is in the foreground. A few of the buildings can be seen in all the photographs, notably Reeves' shop in the left foreground, and the Baptist Chapel of 1866 in Tamworth Road. The 1870 view shows a meadow where Keeley Road and the multi-storey car park are today. Electric trams had arrived by 1910, had been replaced by trolleybuses by 1938, and had reappeared by 1999!

**Views from Town Hall Tower –
   23rd May 1896**
7 Looking South – *opposite top*
Edridge Road, some newly-built houses, and
the spire of St Peter's Church are towards the
right. Coombe Cliff house is in the left
background; woods and downlands can just be
seen in the distance.

8 Looking West – *opposite centre*
The Surrey Street Waterworks is in the right
foreground with the Parish Church beyond.
Smoke is rising from a number of chimneys –
perhaps it was a chilly Spring.

9 Looking North East – *opposite bottom*
The yard behind Hammond and Husseys' High
Street Ironmongery establishment is on the
left. Part of the Fair Field was still being used
for grazing animals behind St. Matthew's
Church, centre. The trees in the background
were in the grounds of Brickwood House.

Views from Town Hall Tower looking East
10 23rd May 1896 – *above*
11 9th September 1999 – *below*
Great changes have taken place during the past
103 years but the water tower on Park Hill
appears in both photographs (top right). The
1896 photographs (illustrations 7, 8, 9 and 10)
appear to have been taken from the very top of
the Town Hall tower on the Saturday after the
building was formally opened by the Prince of
Wales. The 1999 view was taken from a lower
level as can be seen by the chimney in the
foreground, the top of which is below the
photographer in the 1896 view.

Views from Town Hall looking North
12 About 1953 – *above*
13 9th September 1999 – *below*
As on the previous page, the 1950s view is from higher up
in the tower of the Town Hall. It shows the Whitgift Middle
School to the right with St. Michael's Church beyond,
North End runs straight up the centre.

In the 1999 view, St George's Walk has replaced the old
High Street buildings in the foreground, and The Whitgift
Centre is on the school site.

Croydon Airport and Surrey Flying Services

Croydon Aerodrome was established in December 1915 for use by the Royal Flying Corps as part of the Air Defence of London. The actual area used was on the west side on Plough Lane and was at first known as Beddington Aerodrome, or, unofficially, Wallington.

In 1917 three new National Aircraft Factories were planned to increase production of aircraft for the Royal Flying Corps. National Aircraft Factory No.1 was built at Waddon to the east of Plough Lane and a large area was levelled to provide a test flying ground for aircraft built there. This became known as Waddon Aerodrome.

It had become clear during the First World War that flying would be a feature of the new era of peace. Eventually the Government decided that Beddington and Waddon should be used as the airport for London. On 29th March 1920 Croydon Aerodrome as it was by then officially called became the Customs Airport for London.

Initially the old Royal Flying Corps buildings were used as shown in the illustrations on the next page (numbers 16 and 17). As air travel became more popular the Air Ministry decided in 1925 that the airfields on either side of Plough Lane should be combined. The central part of Plough Lane would close, the original buildings would be cleared away, and a new Terminal Building and Hotel would be built on the recently opened Purley Way. The new Airport opened in 1928.

14 Surrey Flying Services Avro 504
Surrey Flying Services was formed in the early 1920s and undertook extensive photographic activities in the locality and much further afield. Many views were published as postcards and most of the 1920s views in this publication were taken by the company. The aircraft used were the famous AVRO 504K type ex First World War as seen here being started. Joy flights at 5/- (25p) were very popular! The company finally merged with the well-known Rollason company.

15 "City of Glasgow" Argosy Aircraft about 1926
The Argosy class of aircraft carried a crew of four and 20 passengers at a speed of up to 105 miles per hour. Here one is seen over Norbury Hill, with a short part of Green Lane just visible in the right corner. The Crystal Palace is just beyond the aircraft, Beulah Hill runs to the right behind the tailplane, and Norwood Grove is towards the bottom left. The remaining open land would shortly be covered by new houses.

16 Croydon Aerodrome – early 1920s
In this view the level crossing over Plough Lane is near top right. The primitive nature of the original aerodrome is apparent.

17 Croydon Aerodrome Main Entrance about 1924
Plough Lane runs across the right of the picture and the *Trust House Hotel* is in the centre.

During the 1920s and 1930s Croydon Airport became famous as the arrival and departure point for many of the great record-breaking flights in civil aviation history. The Royal Air Force took it over in 1939 and it played an important part in the Battle of Britain. It reopened for civil use in 1946 but it was too small for modern aircraft and Gatwick was expanded to replace it. Croydon Airport closed finally in 1959 but its part in the development of civil aviation assures it a place in history.

Croydon Airport Society
The Society was formed in 1978 with the object of perpetuating the history and traditions of Croydon Airport and the men and women who worked and flew from there. The historic records, photographs and memorabilia held by the society are available for local education and for researchers working on British Civil Aviation history.

The Society, now with a membership of over 700 including many from overseas, meets every month at Airport House (the old terminal building).

For further information contact:
Tom Samson
18 Great Woodcote Park
Purley
Surrey CR8 3QS
or Croydon Local Studies Library

18 Croydon Airport about 1929
Shortly after opening, the new Terminal Buildings and Hotel on Purley Way provide a dramatic contrast with the early Plough Lane facilities seen on the opposite page.

19 Croydon Airport – September 1959
Photographed shortly before closure with Purley Way Swimming Pool in the left corner and Waddon Waterworks bottom right.

**20 The Airport and Purley Way – early
   1930s**
Hannibal, one of the famous HP42 aircraft, flies
over Purley Way with the airport in the centre.
The Gas Works can be seen, centre right, with a
great deal of open land remaining to the west.

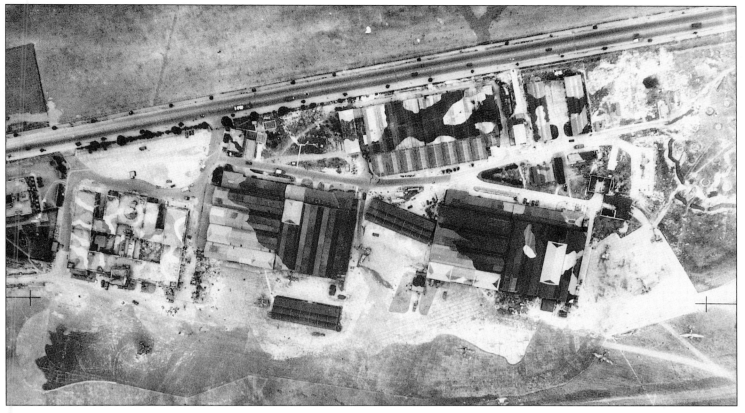

21 Vertical View of Airport – 16th August 1940

This photograph was taken by the RAF Photographic Reconnaissance Unit the day after the German air attack on the airport. Note the camouflage on the roofs.

22 Airport House – 8th January 1993
23 Airport House – 10th January 1997

After Croydon Airport closed in 1959 the Terminal Building was used for commercial purposes. By the 1980s it was in a dilapidated state but was rescued by John Power of Westmead Business Group. It has been restored and is now a thriving International Business Centre and a restaurant.

The petrol station outside rather detracted from its appearance as seen in the 1993 view. By 1997 it had been removed and the forecourt had been landscaped and used for car parking. The De Havilland Heron airliner is a fitting reminder of Croydon Airport's important part in the history of civil aviation. It flew the last scheduled service by Morton Air Services from Croydon to Rotterdam in September 1959.

Aerial Photographs from the 1920s and 1930s

24 Croydon Gas Company's Works – June 1924

This view shows the gas holders and works on the east side of Purley Way. Published by Surrey Flying Services as a postcard, the caption describes it as "shewing crossing of New Motor Road 'Purley Way', over Railway at Northern End". The railway is that from Wimbledon to West Croydon, opened in 1855 over part of the former route of the Surrey Iron Railway. This had opened in 1803 as the world's first public railway, a horse-drawn freight line, which closed in 1846. The line was closed in May 1997 and now forms part of Croydon Tramlink. Note the way in which the former road, Waddon Marsh Lane, had crossed the railway by a level crossing, superseded by the new road bridge. Note also that most of the area was still open land.

25 Thornton Heath Station area about 1924

The Recreation Ground is top centre and Foxley Road is under construction just to the left. Brigstock Road runs from left to right past the station, which had goods yards on both sides. Note the overhead gantries for the electric trains. These were replaced by the present third rail system in 1928.

26 Norbury about 1925
The new police station was under construction just to the north of the railway station. The tram terminus where passengers still had to change between London County Council and Croydon Corporation cars until 1928 is just outside at Hermitage Bridge over the River Graveney, better known locally as the Norbury Brook. This formed the boundary between the ancient parishes of Croydon and Streatham.

The open land to the top right was part of the North Surrey Golf Course, the club house of which is near the top of the picture. It is now Norbury Park.

27 The Convent of the Faithful Virgin, Upper Norwood about 1924
Central Hill runs through the trees from top left to bottom right. This has formed the northern boundary of Croydon Parish for at least 1000 years, Lambeth being to the right. Hermitage Road is at the bottom of the picture. Cattle graze in the Convent grounds. The woodland and open area to the right of Central Hill were developed as a housing estate in the late 1920s.

28 Upper Norwood about 1930
The top of South Norwood Hill is seen (bottom right) with All Saint's Church and its prominent spire (bottom centre), a landmark to this day. Church Road runs straight ahead and the Crystal Palace is in the distance. Formerly part of the Great North Wood, the area is still well-wooded but many of the large houses seen here were demolished and replaced by flats after the 1950s.

29 The Crystal Palace about 1925
The magnificent glass structure dominated South London and North Croydon from 1854 until it was destroyed by fire in 1936. It was not actually in Croydon, but just across the border in Penge. The buildings forming a triangular shape, (bottom centre) are in Croydon. The High Level Railway Station is to the left of the Crystal Palace Parade which runs in front of the Palace.

**30 The Ruins of the Crystal Palace –
1 December 1936**
The fire which engulfed the Crystal Palace was
one of the largest ever seen in the South of
England. Nearly half the strength of London's
fire brigade attended - 89 engines and 381
firemen. The flames at times reached a height
of 300 feet and the fire was visible at Brighton.
This view shows the ruins on the next
morning. The two water towers survived but
were demolished early in the Second World
War as it was thought they were too prominent
a landmark for German bombers.

31 Goat House Bridge, South Norwood about 1924

The main London Bridge to Croydon railway line runs from bottom centre to top right. The overhead electric gantries are clearly visible. The tracks branching to the left linked Norwood Junction and Beckenham Junction but the branch line closed in the 1960s and building has covered much of it. Sunny Bank and Manor Road are to the left, and South Norwood High Street is on the right. The tram tracks appear to be under repair.

32 South Norwood – 1924

The same railway line as above runs from top left to right to Norwood Junction Station. South Norwood Hill runs from near bottom left towards top right. The Stanley Halls and Technical School are to the left of centre and behind the open land is the grounds of Cumberlow, formerly home of William Ford Stanley who donated the halls and school to South Norwood. The Methodist Church is opposite the halls and South Norwood High Street is just beyond.

33 Selhurst Road and Station – 1924

Looking towards South Norwood, Dagnall Park is to the left, and Gloucester Road bottom centre. Holy Trinity Church and Schools are alongside the railway, and beyond the bridge, on the right is the Southern Railway Athletic Club Football Ground. This was formerly *The Nest*, the home of Croydon Common Football Club. Selhurst Railway Depot now covers the site.

34 Selhurst Grammar Schools – 1924
The boys' school is to the left and the girls' to the right. The boys' school is now Selhurst High, and the girls part of the Brit Performing Arts School. A part of Whitehorse Road is on the left. There was still an orchard and open land between The Crescent and Whitehorse Road when this picture was taken.

35 Thornton Heath Pond about 1928
London Road runs from top right to the bottom of the picture. The Pond and its fountain are near the centre. Galpins, Headcorn and Leander Roads are at the top, with Silverleigh and Mayfield Roads to the left. A fair had been set up on land alongside which Fairlands Avenue is under construction - possibly the reason for the naming of the road! The open land is part of the Grove estate now occupied by Goldwell, Ashley, Kirklees and Grove Roads, and Redford Avenue. This picture demonstrates the way in which the remaining open country to the north of Croydon was being developed for housing in the 1920s and 30s. Building is evident in several places. Near the bottom left corner is the tram depot.

36 Whitehorse Road looking towards Thornton Heath – 1924
Spurgeon's Tabernacle and the as yet unwidened bridge are at the bottom. Just to the left of centre is the bell and clock foundry of Gillett and Johnston which closed in the late 1950s and was demolished in the late 1990s. The products of this famous company were sent all over the world. Windmill and Northcote Roads run across the centre at an angle and the *Selhurst Picture Palace* (later the *Luxor Cinema*) can just be seen to the left of Whitehorse Road and below the Recreation Ground. The cinema was destroyed by a flying bomb in 1944.

37 West Croydon Station area – early 1930s.
The 1840s station terminus building with its overall
roof is at the bottom and the present station building
and shops are under construction. North End and
London Road run from top left to bottom right. Trams,
buses and a few cars can be seen.

38 Whitgift Grammar School – 1924
A tram is passing the entrance to the school in North
End. Erected in 1871, the school moved to Haling Park
in 1931 and the building seen here was then used by the
Whitgift Middle (later renamed Trinity) School. This
moved to Shirley Park in 1965 and the buildings and
playing fields were replaced by the Whitgift Centre.

39 The Parish Church and Old Palace – 1924
The Parish Church of St. John the Baptist was almost completely rebuilt following a disastrous fire in 1867. The tower survived and dates from the 14th Century. Most of the pinnacles were removed after the Second World War. The Old Palace to the right was Croydon's Manor House from at least the 11th Century. It was for centuries used by the Archbishops of Canterbury as their near London, country residence. Six are buried in the church. The palace, with recent extensions, has been used as a girl's school since 1887.

40 Wandle Park – 1924
Parts of Kemble and Siddons Roads are at the bottom left. The single track branch line from West Croydon curves away in the foreground towards Wimbledon. It is now part of Tramlink. The footbridges on the left and at the bottom have been removed and a new flyover constructed to take trams across the West Croydon to Sutton railway lines, just off the bottom of this view. Wandle Park was opened in 1890 and its lake was very popular for boating. Unfortunately it proved impossible to maintain the water level after the Second World War and the lake was filled in during the 1960s.

41 George Street about 1924
Looking west, St Matthew's Church is in the centre foreground, with Thrift's Grocery Warehouse and clocktower to the right. The Public Halls, built in 1865, are centre right. The Bovril advert is on a building on the corner of Crown Hill. Compare this picture with illustration number 94 on page 58.

42 London Road – 25th June 1927

Croydon General Hospital is on the left, and West Croydon Wesleyan Methodist Church is top right. The Church was demolished after the Second World War and replaced by a more modest structure. The South Suburban Co-operative Society's new head offices and store is on the right. This was demolished in the 1980s. The crowds had gathered to welcome King George V and Queen Mary on their visit to the hospital to view the new extension which had been opened earlier in the afternoon by the Archbishop of Canterbury, Dr. Randall Davidson.

43 Aurelia Road about 1926

Thornton Road runs from left to right across the top of the picture and Aurelia Road is near the bottom, with some new houses under construction. Croydon Cemetery is in the bottom left corner and its later extension now has the main entrance just to the left of the bend in Thornton Road. Houses can also be seen being built in Harcourt Road (top centre). The large factory is that of The Accounting and Tabulating Corporation Ltd (later Powers Samas). This view provides another graphic illustration of how the remaining open land to the north of Croydon was being built over between the wars.

44 East Croydon Station about 1924
Several of the houses in Altyre Road (bottom left) still exist but otherwise virtually all the buildings seen here have been demolished since the 1960s. The station building dated from the mid 1890s when it replaced the earlier station which had entrances from either side, not the bridge. The present station building replaced that seen here in 1991.

45 Fairfield about 1930
East Croydon Station is just visible top left, with St Matthew's Church just below. Park Lane is near the bottom, with Katharine Street and the Town Hall Gardens bottom right. Fairfield was bought by the London Brighton and South Coast Railway for the construction of their Central Croydon branch in the 1860s. The tracks continued under Park Lane and the Town Hall Gardens were laid out in the cutting after the station closed in 1890. The Town Hall occupies the site of the station. After gravel extraction, the railway company built sidings and workshops on Fairfield and used them until the early 1930s. The site was then acquired by Croydon Corporation and the new Technical College, School of Art, and Fairfield Halls were built on the site from the mid 1950s onwards.

46 High Street looking North about 1927
The Town Hall was the most conspicuous landmark
in the town until the redevelopment of the 1960s.

The Grand Theatre is just below centre right and
next door is Nalder and Collyer's Brewery, one of
three then in the town.

47 Shirley Schools about 1924

The Bermondsey Poor Law Guardians erected the schools in 1903 on the site of Shirley Lodge Farm. There were 37 detached houses, school, laundry, technical training centre and water pumping station, the tower of which is towards top centre. The grounds covered 79 acres. The London County Council took over the schools in 1920 and after closure in the 1980s new housing and Shirley Oaks Hospital have been built in the grounds.

48 Water Tower, Park Hill about 1924

The Water Tower was built in 1867 to provide better water pressure from the adjacent reservoir (built in 1851) to new housing on the nearby high ground. The park, formerly part of the Archbishops of Canterbury's Deer Park, was opened in 1888. Until the Second World War the tower was used as a viewing point (see illustration 97).

49 Shirley Park Hotel – Early 1930s

Addiscombe Road and the Golf Club House are at the bottom and Upper Shirley Road runs from bottom left to top left. Shirley Windmill is just visible to the right. The hotel was formerly Shirley House, a splendid Georgian building which was replaced by the Trinity School of John Whitgift in the mid 1960s. It seems a pity the old mansion could not have been incorporated in the fine modern school.

50 Addington Village – 1938

As yet unaffected by modern development, Addington until the 1960s remained a rural enclave, only three miles from the town centre. The Church of St Mary is the burial place of five Archbishops of Canterbury who used nearby Addington Palace as a rural retreat during the 19th century. Spout Hill is to the right and Lodge Lane bottom right. New Addington was already under construction and partly occupied at this time and the private bus which linked it with the 64 bus route terminus at Featherbed Lane is just visible.

51 Swan and Sugar Loaf area about 1924
The well-known landmark on the Brighton Road is just below right of centre. Open-top buses can be seen standing on its forecourt. St. Peter's Church with its prominent spire is towards the top centre. The main Brighton railway line and South Croydon Station are at the top.

52 Red Deer area about 1924
Another well-known landmark on the Brighton Road, the public house is centre left, again with buses on the forecourt. Sanderstead Road runs across the left of the picture, and St. Augustine's Avenue runs from opposite the back of the pub to the bottom right hand corner. St. Augustine's Church, built in 1883, is just to the right with Churchill Road behind.

53 Waddon Estate about 1928
Denning Avenue runs from centre left to top
left with Cosedge Crescent on the left and
Layton and Crowley Crescents on the right.
Purley Way is in the foreground with
Coldharbour Road beyond. Construction of the
Corporation estate by Perry Brothers started in
the mid 1920s.

54 Purley in the early 1930s
Banstead Road is to the left with Russell Hill
Road and Purley Way towards the centre top.
Brighton Road runs from bottom left towards
top right with High Street curving down
towards bottom right. The Waterworks (now the
site of Tesco) is at the bottom.

55 New Addington about 1936
The first houses in New Addington were built by the Henry Boot Company in the mid 1930s. Building work ceased at the outbreak of the Second World War and most of the township was built afterwards by Croydon Corporation between the 1940s and the 1960s. In this view Parkway runs from the large roundabout towards Central Parade which is just off the picture to the right of centre. Beyond Parkway is Montacute Road with Gascoigne Road and, from right to left, Heneage Crescent, Bothwell and Grenville Roads, Shaxton, Aldrich, and Wolsey Crescents. Note the almost complete lack of trees.

56 Croham Heights about 1926
The Royal Russell School and Ballards Way are in the background. Addington Road runs from bottom left towards centre right. Upper Selsdon Road is on the left with Queenhill Road running across Farley Road towards Littleheath Woods. Byron, Rylandes, and the first part of Littleheath Roads are also in the picture.

57 Selsdon Looking South – 1935
Upper Selsdon Road runs from bottom left to centre right with Addington Road from centre right to top left. This picture was taken about ten years after that on the opposite page (illustration 56) and the area had already matured noticeably. New buildings can be seen in the Sundale Avenue and Selsdon Vale areas, but there was still a great deal of open land towards Addington.

58 Sanderstead Looking North – 1935
Limpsfield Road and Borough Farm are on the left with the pond, church and Selsdon Court just below the centre. Addington Road runs from just below centre right to the top of Sanderstead Hill which curves away through the trees to the north with Purley Beeches on the left. The newly laid-out roads to the right are The Woodfields, The Windings, Farm Fields and Sundown Avenue. On the left the first short part of Rectory Park is there and Glebe Hyrst, Brian Avenue and adjacent roads have been newly built.

59 Coulsdon about 1924
Smitham Station is just off the bottom of the
picture and the railway curves round to pass
under Woodcote Grove Road at the top.
Brighton Road runs from bottom right to top
left, with Chipstead Valley Road turning off to
left of top centre. Malcolm Road is on the right
and the *Coulsdon Cinema* can be seen on the
bend. Edward Road and the Waterworks are on
the left. The area was known as Smitham
Bottom until the early 20th century, Old
Coulsdon being the original ancient settlement
and only being called 'Old' from the 1920s.

60 Smitham Downs about 1924
Brighton Road is in the foreground with Smitham
Downs Road curving away to the left beyond The
Drive. This is a good illustration of the way in
which the downs to the south of Croydon were
gradually being covered by 'desirable residences'
in the period between the wars.

61 Old Coulsdon – early 1930s
Coulsdon Road runs from centre left to just below top right with Court Avenue under construction in the foreground. The Parish Church of St John is on the extreme right and Bradmore Green is near the top right corner beyond Grange Park Recreation Ground. Placehouse Lane runs from the newly built parade of shops past Purley County School towards the left.

62 Marlpit Lane, Coulsdon – May 1929
Looking south-east, the bottom part of Marlpit Lane had been widened but the top part was still a narrow country lane leading up to Bradmore Green. On the left Marlpit Avenue, Coulsdon Rise and the first part of Stoneyfield Road are there, while on the right Hillside Road and Bradmore Way are being cut in the chalk downland. A short section of Chaldon Way has also been laid out.

The Story of Handford Photography

63 Archie Handford

Archie was a keen radio 'Ham' and is seen here with some of his wireless equipment. When he first started his George Street business he lived over the shop but later moved to Purley. He was active in the Home Guard during the Second World War. He died in 1979.

64 Paul Proctor

Paul Proctor of Chorley Handford photographed with his camera ready for action. Paul came south from Sheffield and has lived in the Croydon area for nearly 40 years. He served in the RAF in Singapore for three years and has always worked as a photographer, spending a

short time with the old Croydon firm of Durbin and McBryde in North End. He is an Associate of the British Institute of Photographers and of the Royal Photographic Society.

65 Tom Samson

Tom Samson awaiting take off with his Medium Format camera for which he always uses colour negative film. He has lived in the Wallington area since he was six years old and has a lifelong involvement with the scout movement. He worked closely for many years with Croydon Advertising Association and the Croydon Chamber of Commerce. He is Chairman of the Croydon Airport Society.

Archie Handford started business in Croydon in 1921 with a studio at 62 George Street. He dealt mainly with portraits and weddings. In the 1930s he expanded the business with commercial photography for the developing industries in the Croydon area. As a specialist field he undertook 16mm cine photography making films for the Croydon Gas Company and also for the Nestlé Company on the making of their new product - Condensed Milk.

Tom Samson joined the firm as a trainee in 1937. His photographic career was interrupted by service in the RAF from 1942 to 1946 when he served as a navigator on Transport Command Dakotas in the Far East. Returning to the business in 1946 he decided to combine a photographic and flying career. In the post-war boom of re-construction he developed extensive aerial photography contracts with major companies such as McAlpine, Taylor Woodrow and Costain. The start of this was the building of the new Croydon 'B' Power Station and continuing to cover the first nuclear power station at Bradwell. The development of Gatwick then followed over many years. Even today, the firm covers developments at Gatwick and all the other BAA airports.

Archie Handford retired and a company was formed with Leslie Carter, Robert Pyke, and David Perks as Directors. The business continued to grow and became a major force covering aerial photography of construction projects including the London Docklands development. A picture library of this historic work was established. Around 1970 the firm merged with the old established architectural photographers, Bedford Lemére and Company.

With rising rents in George Street it was decided to concentrate on commercial and industrial photography based on the studio at 1A South Park Hill Road. Tom Samson was active in the British Institute of Professional Photography and was elected National President in 1969. In 1971 an exhibition to celebrate 50 years of the business was staged at Fairfield Halls.

Tom Samson decided to retire in 1988 and the business was merged with the photography and laboratory company, Chorley Hyman and Rose Ltd, run by Peter Chorley and Paul Proctor in Wallington. The company now operates as Chorley Handford at 129A Stafford Road, Wallington. Paul Proctor undertakes all flying and the picture library has been expanded to around 100,000 photographs. These cover much of the United Kingdom and include major construction projects such as Canary Wharf, the Channel Tunnel Terminal, the Millennium Dome, many town centres and all principal football stadia. Internet service brings enquiries for stock library pictures from worldwide sources.

Photographs from the 1950s to 1999

66 Croydon Town Hall – 2nd August 1991
This photograph is a good example of the work of Chorley Handford in recording construction work in progress. Work had just started on the new Library and Clocktower complex and a tower crane is on site. The 1851 Waterworks building at the back of Surrey Street was boarded up – it has since been nicely restored. The vacant site alongside is now occupied by Surrey Street multi-storey car park and the former Grants' store building is under reconstruction and restoration for new purposes.

67 London Road – 13th April 1984
The spire of the former West Croydon Congregational Church on the corner of Campbell Road is still a landmark although somewhat dwarfed by Concord House on the opposite corner. Broad Green Avenue is behind Concord House, and in the foreground from right to left are Fairholme and Greenside Roads, Midhurst Avenue and Canterbury Road. Note the wide variety of house styles typical of many parts of Croydon that were developed over a long period of years. There are also many light industrial and commercial premises.

68 London Road about 1924
There were many more trees to be seen in 1924 and the roads were not cluttered with parked cars. Midhurst Avenue had not yet been built and there was still open land behind Campbell Road. This had been used as smallholdings at one time.

69 Addiscombe Station – 28th July 1992
The station, originally Croydon (Addiscombe Road), was opened in 1864 by the South Eastern Railway who extended their Mid Kent line from Beckenham. They really wanted to have a town centre terminus but this was as near as they could get. The area to the right was formerly an extensive goods yard. The station was closed in May 1997 as part of the Tramlink project but by then the train depot on the left had been closed and the station saw only a solitary two-car train at any one time. Lower Addiscombe Road runs from left to right near the top of the picture. Warren and Hastings Roads are on the right, with part of Grant Road on the left.

70 Selhurst Looking South – 26th May 1999

New houses have been built on former railway land at the back of Davidson Road to the left of the tracks. Tennyson Road is in the foreground. The full extent of Selhurst Railway Depot and the complicated track layout is visible. The tracks leading to East Croydon continue towards the top centre and those to West Croydon towards the top right following the original alignment of the Croydon Canal which closed in 1836. Note the dense woodland that has grown up near the depot since the 1985 picture on the next page (illustration 71). Lower Addiscombe and St. James's Roads are just visible running across the picture in the distance where Windmill Bridge crosses the railway by the two tower blocks.

71 Selhurst Looking North – 1985
Davidson Road is in the foreground and Northcote and Selhurst Roads cross from near top left to top right. Selhurst Station and the Railway Depot are top right. This photograph was taken soon after major works had been carried out in the area to provide a new track layout with additional flyovers. Compare it with the view on the previous page taken 14 years later.

**72 Coulsdon and The North Downs –
   9th July 1991**
The centre of Coulsdon is bottom left and Chipstead Valley Road runs across from left to right about a quarter of a way up the picture. Farthing Downs and Devilsden Wood are towards top left, and Cane Hill Hospital is just above centre right. How fortunate Croydonians are to have such attractive Green Belt countryside on the doorstep.

**73 Croydon 'B' Power Station –
9th September 1983**
Designed and built by Croydon Corporation,
the Power Station came into use in 1947. It is
seen here at the time of its closure and, apart
from the chimneys, it has since been
demolished. Waddon Isolation Hospital is to
the centre right.

**74 Ikea and Purley Way –
5th November 1992**
Nine years later the area had already changed a
lot. The six cooling towers had been replaced
by commercial buildings and the Isolation
Hospital was making way for new housing.
The Swedish company, Ikea, had opened their
massive retail store and it was already causing
traffic problems. In the subsequent seven years

the fields to the left of Ikea have been covered
by more retail warehouses and a large multi-
screen cinema. This area was a part of Waddon
Marsh but is now known as Valley Park. The
office block (top right) has been demolished
and the railway line is now part of Tramlink,
with its new depot where the trees are just
beyond the chimneys.

75 Addington Palace – 27th May 1999
For many years from the 1950s Addington Palace was the home of the Royal School of Church Music. It has recently been well restored and is used as a Conference Centre with a Restaurant and Fitness Club. The large cedar tree in front is one of the great trees of England and is over 200 years old. The grounds of the palace were laid out by 'Capability' Brown the famous landscape architect. See also illustration 50 on page 29.

76 Whitgift School, Haling Park – 15th May 1990
Nottingham Road curves round in the left bottom corner with Whitgift Avenue running across to the right. The original 1931 school buildings are set around the quadrangle to the left and the others are more recent additions. Haling Park was the home of Lord Howard of Effingham, England's High Admiral at the time of the Spanish Armada. He died here and was buried at Reigate. The open space is a welcome break in this urban part of South Croydon.

77 Roman Way Looking North – 8th April 1976
The Old Town and Pitlake areas were transformed by the construction of the town's western relief road, at the time intended to be part of a complete inner ring road, of which the flyover and Wellesley Road are part. Here the road is still being built, with the Parish Church and Old Palace on the right. The Tamworth Road multi-storey car park is near the top right corner.

**78 Purley Way and Gas Works –
   8th March 1966**
Waddon Mill is in the foreground, with
Waddon Ponds to the right. Purley Way runs
from top left to centre right. The massive
Philips factory is centre left. In 1966 this was
Croydon's main manufacturing area but
warehouses and superstores such as
Sainsbury's and Habitat have replaced most of
the factories. Compare this photograph with
illustration number 24 on page 14.

79 Town Centre Looking West – July 1959
The new Technical College was being built on
Fairfield with open car parking still alongside.
The layout of the spaces was obviously
influenced by the railway track layout seen in
illustration 45 on page 26! The back of the
massive *Davis Theatre* building is centre left
and George Street runs from bottom right to
the centre. The pre-war Gas and Electricity
Board offices were the only notable office
blocks apart from the recently-built Norfolk
House on the corner of Wellesley Road. The
playing fields of the Trinity School of John
Whitgift were a welcome green space in the
town, now covered by the Whitgift Centre. In
the distance the Gas Works and Croydon 'A'
and 'B' Power Stations provide an industrial
backdrop.

80 Town Centre – 5th February 1964
By this time the 1960s redevelopment of the
town centre was well under way. The Fairfield
Halls had opened, the Gas Board offices were
dwarfed by St George's House, centre left, the
Technical College was virtually complete and
new offices were appearing behind Norfolk
House (top right). Trinity School was as yet
untouched by the Whitgift Centre project and
the Park Lane underpass was being built. The
general mess and disruption caused by the
massive roadworks in the 1960s and 1970s
were the object of far less complaint than the
recent Tramlink works!

**81 The Flyover From Impact House –
    8th May 1967**
The girders for the new flyover had just been placed in position but it would be some time before it opened to relieve east-west traffic. The old Swimming Baths in Scarbrook Road and adjacent almshouses (both now gone) are in the background.

**82 Town Centre Looking North East –
    29th March 1968**
The Whitgift Centre office towers were being built but several tall blocks had still to appear when this picture was taken. The High Street and Old Town Flyover is well under way and the town had already earned its title of a Mini-Manhattan.

**83 The Town Hall from St. George's House
    – 9th May 1963**
The fine Victorian Town Hall is seen to special effect here. There were serious thoughts of demolishing it by the late 1960s but fortunately older buildings were beginning to be appreciated and it has now been well-restored both internally and externally. The rather fine 1860s terrace opposite in Katharine Street however was destroyed soon after this picture was taken and replaced by rather ordinary offices. The *Davis Theatre* had already been replaced by Davis House, left and, Green Dragon House nearly opposite had replaced the historic hostelry of that name. Croydon was already changing rapidly.

84 Park Hill – 15th March 1972
Massive changes during the 1960s were not just confined to the town centre. Many of the large Victorian houses in Upper Norwood and parts of Croydon were on 99 year leases which ran out during the 60s. Park Hill was almost totally redeveloped by Wates as Park Hill Village. Addiscombe Road runs across the centre, Park Hill Road is on the left, Park Hill Rise to the right, and Chepstow Road in the foreground. Nearly 30 years later the landscaping has given the area a pleasantly mature appearance but it all looked rather bare and new in 1972.

86 Royal Russell School – 12th June 1968
The Warehousemen and Drapers' school at Ballards Plantation was provided as an addition to the Russell Hill School at Purley in 1921. The extension to the original building was designed by Sir Aston Webb, architect of the frontage of Buckingham Palace. The school was formally opened by HRH Prince of Wales in 1924. Ballards Way is on the right.

85 Shirley Park – 13th February 1981
Shirley and Upper Shirley Roads run from top centre to bottom right with Addiscombe Road to the left centre. Compare this with the photograph on page 29 (illustration 49). The Trinity School of John Whitgift was moved from North End in 1965 and the new buildings seen here have subsequently been extended.

87 New Addington Centre – 23rd
September 1964
Central Parade is in the middle with Salcot
Crescent on the right and Overbury Crescent
on the left. Parkway and the Community
centre are towards the top right. Featherbed
Lane is on the extreme left and Addington
Palace can just be seen in the distance (top
right). The area all looked rather new and
lacking in vegetation. Thirty years later it has
matured nicely.

88 New Addington – Fieldway –
24th July 1967
Fieldway was the last part of New Addington
to be built and was nearing completion at the
time of this photograph. Dunley Drive which
runs from top right to bottom right, and the
area to the right was built earlier. The
woodland is Birch Wood Ruff, part of the
ancient boundary between Surrey and Kent.
Addington Village Road, now renamed Kent
Gate Way, runs across the top left corner with
Three Halfpenny Wood beyond.

89 Beaulieu Heights Upper Norwood –
22nd July 1991
Originally part of the Great North Wood the
land later formed part of two estates,
Hazelwood and Beaulieu Lodge. The large
house was later used as a hotel and in recent
years as an old peoples home. The aerial was
originally the main ITV transmitter. South
Norwood Hill runs from near bottom left to
the junction with Upper Beulah Hill and
Church Road to the right. All Saint's Church
was built in 1827 when the ancient Parish of
Croydon was divided up to cope with a
growing population.

90 Purley Cross – 29th November 1985
The main Brighton railway line runs from centre left towards top right. The Caterham branch curves away to the centre top and the Tattenham Corner branch is between that and the main line. The old South Eastern Railway locomotive shed is still there but used for other purposes since the 1920s. The East Surrey Water Company's works are prominent. Purley and Godstone Roads are to the left and Brighton Road is in the foreground.

91 Purley Cross – 10th September 1992
Seven years after illustration 90, the Waterworks has been replaced by a large Tesco store and major road improvements have brought a new gyratory system into operation. The old Railway Hotel on the corner of the High Street (seen in the earlier picture, extreme left) has been replaced by a new office block.

92 Taberner House, Town Hall and Fairfield – 26th May 1999
Old Town and Roman Way are at the top with High Street running across the centre. The new addition to the back of the Town Hall on which work had just started in illustration 66 on page 37 was completed in 1993. Now known as the *Clocktower*, the splendid addition to the town's facilities includes one of the largest libraries in the country, a museum and the *David Lean Cinema*.

93 The Town Centre – 26th May 1999
This striking view shows Wellesley Road and Park Lane on the right, with the Police Station, Fairfield Halls and Croydon College towards the bottom. North End and High Street are just to the left of centre and part of Mitcham Road and Roman Way are top left. Tramlink works are under way in Wellesley Road.

**94 George Street and Park Lane –
26th May 1999**
Croydon College and Suffolk House are at the
bottom with St. George's House, centre, and
the Town Hall, now known as the *Clocktower*
towards top left. George Street runs from the
bottom towards top right. Tramlink works can
be seen in progress.

**95 East Croydon Station –
3rd September 1992**
The new Station building is not universally
admired but has won design awards and is an
imaginative concept for a difficult site. The
bridge over the railway consists of several
different structures and could not support the
weight of an adequate building. It has therefore
been built on similar lines to a suspension
bridge and is supported by four towers.
See illustration 44 page 26.

**96 East Croydon Station –
1st September 1999**
A more recent view of the station shows the
new Tramlink station on the bridge outside is
almost complete. The NLA tower, locally
known as the 'Threepeny bit building' is in the
foreground.

**97 View from Park Hill Water Tower
– 24th October 1971**

This view is looking west with St. George's House and Fairfield Halls on the right and Taberner House towards the left. The Water Tower on Park Hill has been a well-known local landmark for 130 years. Between the wars it was a popular viewpoint for local residents but after the Second World War it was not reopened to the public. By the late 1960s it had become unsafe and the interior was demolished in the early 1970s leaving it as just a shell. A small party of members of the Croydon Natural History and Scientific Society made a final visit in October 1971, when this picture was taken.

**98 Old Palace from Parish Church Tower –
6th September 1999**

For centuries Croydon's Manor House and the country home of the Archbishops of Canterbury, Croydon Palace was sold in 1780 and after becoming a factory, was restored as a school in 1887. Much of the Palace remains as shown by the view from above. It is now part of the Whitgift Foundation and is one of the town's greatest historical and architectural treasures.

It is a pity that so few people can enjoy the pleasures of viewing their town from above. Locally the splendid views from the Norwood Hills or from the downs and other higher parts of the town are in many cases quite spectacular: but on Addington Hills and Croham Hurst, encroaching vegetation, particularly Silver Birch trees, has obscured most of the views for which these spots were once so famous. Several of our office blocks have viewing galleries but special arrangements have to be made to obtain access. It is to be hoped that in the 21st century more will be done to enable residents and visitors to enjoy the vistas that Addington Hills, Croham Hurst and some of the tall buildings could provide.

For the last few illustrations (numbers 97 and 98 opposite), and inside the back cover (numbers 99 and 100), we return from aerial views to take a look from a couple of our older high buildings.

The Water Tower on Park Hill was a very popular venue earlier in the 20th Century and as shown in illustration 97 opposite provided a good view of the town; also its surroundings, south to the downs, east towards Shooters Hill, and north to the Norwood Hills and beyond. It is not inconceivable that one day the present empty shell could be be put to some useful purpose and the top again be made available as a viewing point.

The Parish Church tower dates from the 14th Century and fortunately escaped the disastrous fire that engulfed the church in 1867. It cannot be made accessible to the public, but no doubt quite a few Croydonians, bell-ringers, and church officials have, over the past 700 years climbed the same steep stairs to look out on their changing town. Until little more than 150 years ago they would have seen fields, woods and streams to the north, west and south. To the east they would have seen the town that John Ruskin alluded to in 1885. "......it is evident to me in retrospect.....that the personal feeling and native instinct of me had been fastened irrevocably long before to things modest, humble and pure in peace, under the low red roofs of Croydon, and by the cress set rivulets in which the sand danced and the minnows darted above the springs of Wandel." John Ruskin would certainly not recognise that Croydon today!

Bibliography

The information in this publication has been obtained from many sources. For the reader wishing to study in more depth the development of the Croydon area during the past, the following are recommended.

Anderson, J. Corbet — *A CHRONICLE OF CROYDON*, Ballantyne Press, 1882. Republished by SR Publishers Ltd, 1970.

Anderson, J. Corbet — *CROYDON INCLOSURE*, Printed for the Subscribers, 1889.

Baddeley, G.E. — *THE TRAMWAYS OF CROYDON* (Revised Edition), The Light Rail Transit Association, 1983.

Beaver, Patrick — *THE CRYSTAL PALACE*, Philimore, 1986.

Berwick Sayers, W.C. — *SAMUEL COLERIDGE-TAYLOR - MUSICIAN - HIS LIFE AND LETTERS*, Cassell, 1915.

Berwick Sayers, W.C. (Ed) — *CROYDON AND THE SECOND WORLD WAR*, The Croydon Corporation, 1949.

Broadbent, U. and Latham, R. (Ed) — *COULSDON, DOWNLAND VILLAGE*, The Bourne Society, 1976.

Clenet, Deidre; Britton, Bob and Game, Meg — *NATURE CONSERVATION IN CROYDON*, London Ecology Unit, 1988.

Cluett, Douglas; Nash, Joanna and Learmonth, Bob — *CROYDON AIRPORT. THE GREAT DAYS*, 1928-1939, Sutton Libraries and Arts Services, 1980.

Croydon Advertiser — *CROYDON ADVERTISER 1869-1969*, *Croydon Advertiser*, 1969.

Croydon Advertiser — *JESSE WARD*, *Croydon Advertiser*, 1951

Croydon Advertiser — *OLD AND NEW CROYDON ILLUSTRATED 1894*, Republished by *Croydon Advertiser*, 1979.

The Croydon Society and Croydon Council — *CROYDON'S LIVING HERITAGE*, The Croydon Society and Croydon Council, 1995.

Eyles, Allen and Skone, Keith — *THE CINEMAS OF CROYDON*, Keytone Publications in association with Croydon Public Libraries, 1989.

Gent, John B. — *CROYDON, A PICTORIAL HISTORY*, Phillimore & Co. Ltd., 1991.

Gent, John B. (Ed) — *CROYDON BETWEEN THE WARS*, Croydon Natural History and Scientific Society. Second Edition, 1992.

Gent, John B. (Ed) — *CROYDON IN THE 1940s AND 1950s*, Croydon Natural History and Scientific Society, 1994.

Gent, John B. (Ed) — *CROYDON OLD AND NEW*, Croydon Natural History and Scientific Society. Fourth Edition, 1996.

Gent, John B. (Ed) — *CROYDON, THE STORY OF A HUNDRED YEARS*, Croydon Natural History and Scientific Society. Sixth Edition, 1988.

Gent, John B. (Ed) — *EDWARDIAN CROYDON ILLUSTRATED*, Croydon Natural History and Scientific Society. Second Edition, 1990.

Gent, John B. (Ed) — *VICTORIAN CROYDON ILLUSTRATED*, Croydon Natural History and Scientific Society. Second Edition, 1987.

Learmonth, Bob; Nash, Joanna and Cluett, Douglas (Ed) — *THE FIRST CROYDON AIRPORT*, 1915-1928, Sutton Libraries and Arts Services, 1977.

McInnes, Paula and Sparkes, Bill — *CROYDON AT WORK*, The Croydon Society and Croydon Chamber of Commerce and Industry, 1991.

Moore, Ald. H. Keatley and Berwick Sayers, W.C. (Ed) — *CROYDON AND THE GREAT WAR*, Libraries Committee of the Corporation of Croydon, 1920.

Paget, Clarence G. — *BY-WAYS IN THE HISTORY OF CROYDON*, Croydon Public Libraries, 1929.

Paget, Clarence G. — *CROYDON HOMES OF THE PAST*, Croydon Public Libraries, 1937.

Pelton, John O. — *RELICS OF OLD CROYDON*, Roffey and Clark, 1891.

Percy, F.H.G. — *WHITGIFT SCHOOL, A HISTORY*, The Whitgift Foundation, 1991.

Skinner, M.W.G. — *CROYDON'S RAILWAYS*, Kingfisher Railway Productions, 1985.

Thornhill, Lilian — *CONSERVATION AREAS OF CROYDON*, Croydon Society, 1987.

Warwick, Alan R. — *THE PHOENIX SUBURB*, Blue Boar Press, 1972.

Winterman, M.A. — *CROYDON'S PARKS, An Illustrated History*, London Borough of Croydon, 1988.

Local directories published by Gray, Warren and Ward from 1851 onwards are invaluable sources of information and in addition local newspapers are very useful contemporary sources. Croydon has had about 60 since the mid-nineteenth century. The best are the *Croydon Chronicle* (from 1855) and the *Croydon Advertiser* (from 1869). In using local newspapers it should however be borne in mind that reports may be politically or otherwise biased.

The Croydon Natural History and Scientific Society has published Proceedings and Transactions since 1871, and some of these contain useful local historical information on the period.

The Bourne Society has published Local History Records annually since 1962 and these include articles on the southern districts.

Living History Publications and North Downs Press have also produced some very useful publications.

The Local Studies Library in Katharine Street holds copies of these and many other publications for reference purposes.

Acknowledgements

The illustrations are from the following sources and are reproduced by their kind permission. In some cases it has not been possible to trace the photographer or holder of the copyright, but their contribution is nevertheless gratefully acknowledged.

Chorley Handford — Frontispiece and numbers 22, 23, 63, 64, 65, 66, 67, 69, 70, 71, 72, 73, 74, 75, 76, 77, 78, 79, 80, 81, 82, 83, 84, 85, 86, 87, 88, 89, 90, 91, 92, 93, 94, 95, 96 and Back Cover.

(Copies of the Chorley Handford photographs can be ordered direct from the company at 129A, Stafford Road, Wallington. The number and title of the illustration should be quoted).

Croydon Airport Society — Numbers 16, 18, 19 and 21.

Croydon Local Studies Library — Numbers 3, 7, 8, 9, 10, 25, 26, 28, 31, 32, 33, 35, 37, 42, 43, 45, 46, 50, 54, 57, 58 and 62.

John Gent — Front Cover and numbers 6, 11, 13, 97, 98, 99 and 100.

John Gent Collection — Numbers 1, 2, 4, 5, 12, 14, 15, 17, 20, 24, 27, 29, 30, 34, 36, 38, 39, 40, 41, 44, 47, 48, 49, 51, 52, 53, 55, 56, 59, 60, 61 and 68.

The Editors and the Council of CNHSS also gratefully acknowledge the help of the following in the production of this publication: **Graham Donaldson, Paul Proctor, Dave Smith (Memories of Hendon), Steve Roud and the staff of Croydon Local Studies Library.**

Old Photographs, Postcards, Maps, Documents and other items of local interest

Croydon Local Studies Library, or the Society would appreciate the donation or loan of items of local interest. Anyone able to assist is requested to write to the Local Studies Librarian or the Secretary of CNHSS.

CNHSS

The Croydon Natural History and Scientific Society

THE SOCIETY'S EMBLEM (left) Based on a bronze open-work disc found in 1893 in a Saxon cemetery in Edridge Road between Croydon High Street and Park Lane. It is a rare example of a 5th or 6th century girdle ornament or amulet and now forms part of the Croydon Clocktower collection.

By 1870, the population of Croydon had reached 50,000 and in March that year, a group of local professional men met to establish **The Croydon Microscopical Club**. The inaugural meeting was held on 6 April 1870 at the Public Halls in George Street, which was to be the Society's home for many years. The initial 80 members included most of the local doctors and many prominent townspeople.

The club soon widened its activities to include photography and other interests, changing its name to **The Croydon Microscopical and Natural History Club** in 1877 and to its present title in 1902. By this time the Society was actively campaigning for a museum in the town.

In 1912, Christopher Fagg initiated the Regional Survey of Croydon and District, widely copied in the 1920s and 1930s with a strong influence on the teaching of geography and some influence in town planning concepts.

The Croydon Natural History and Scientific Society survived two world wars and has maintained publication of its Journal (Proceedings and Transactions of CNHSS) from 1871 to the present.

In 1975 the Society was instrumental in establishing **The Croydon Society** to deal with general town planning and conservation issues.

In 1971 Walter Bennett, a member since 1923, died and left his collections to CNHSS forming the basis of the Society's museum of archaeological, geological, local history and ethnographical artefacts, some of which form part of the collections of Croydon Clocktower. The Society's collections are available for inspection and research by arrangement with the curator.

CNHSS also maintain an extensive reference library for study purposes and with a few exceptions books are available to members on loan.

The Society organises occasional exhibitions and displays at a variety of events. There are opportunities for members to involve themselves in a number of ways or simply to learn more about the natural and local history of Croydon and beyond.

CNHSS is the longest established local voluntary organisation in Croydon

- has published Proceedings since 1871
- was involved in establishing Croydon Camera club in 1890
- helped set up the Photographic Survey & Record of Surrey in 1902
- helped to save Croham Hurst from redevelopment
- helped to save the Whitgift Hospital from demolition
- established the Regional Survey of Croydon and District in 1912
- was involved in setting up Croydon Astronomical Society
- initiated the Croydon Society in 1975
- has published seven illustrated local history books since 1970
- arranges around 80 meetings and visits each year
- has around 450 members
- has consistently campaigned for a Croydon museum
- is a company limited by guaranteed without share capital
- is a registered charity recognised by Croydon Education Authority
- is an educational body
- has a national reputation
- has been awarded a Millennium Lottery Grant to establish a 'Museum without walls' Heritage Trail at stops on the new Croydon Tramlink system

The Society has eight sections, each of which arranges its own programme.

ARCHAEOLOGY Occasional assistance is given with professional archaeological digs. Lectures are held on local and national topics with visits to sites of special interest.

BOTANY Regular lectures and field meetings including recording schemes and conservation projects. The Croydon area has some interesting botanical rarities.

ENTOMOLOGY Regular members' evenings are held and individual member's fieldwork is contributing to the study of insect distribution in Surrey.

GEOLOGY Regular lectures and visits on a wide range of geological interests of South East England and further afield.

Members of the Society are entitled to attend the meetings of all sections.

INDUSTRIAL STUDIES Croydon and the south east is rich in sites of industrial archaeological and transport interest. Lectures and visits are arranged, throughout the year.

LOCAL HISTORY The Croydon area has a varied and interesting history. Lectures and walks are arranged and assistance given with research for the Society's publications.

METEOROLOGY Occasional meetings are held which continue the society's pioneering studies of local weather during the 19th Century.

ORNITHOLOGY Lectures and field meetings covering sites and topics of ornithological interest in Croydon, the south east generally and worldwide.

CNHSS OBJECTIVES:

To encourage the study of the sciences especially the natural and local history and archaeology of the Croydon area by organising lectures, members talks, discussions, exhibitions, outdoor meetings, visits and surveys, by issuing publications and by maintaining a library and a museum.

The Society is concerned with original investigation, conservation, curation, education and incidental recreation.

WHY NOT JOIN NOW AND HELP US IN OUR LOCAL EFFORTS?

WE WELCOME NEW MEMBERS

Croydon Natural History & Scientific Society
96A Brighton Road
South Croydon
Surrey CR2 6AD

CNHSS Publications

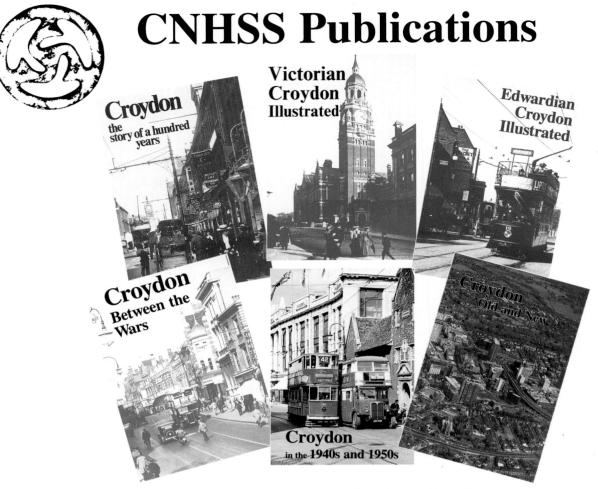

Croydon, the story of a hundred years

First published in 1970 this well-illustrated book gives a general picture of Croydon and the way in which it developed from 1870. It includes sections on Croydon up to 1870, Living Memory, Urban Growth, Transport, Shopping and Commerce, Industry, Municipal Progress, Middle Row, Education, Church and Charity, Leisure, The Redevelopment Boom of the 1960s, and Croydon since 1970. A sixth edition was published in 1988. A few copies remain in stock - only available on order by post.

Victorian Croydon Illustrated

First published in 1979, this includes over 100 illustrations of Croydon during the Victorian period, from the early days of photography to 1901. It was the first publication in a series which will reproduce some of the more interesting photographs from various periods of Croydon's past. A second edition was published in 1987.

Edwardian Croydon Illustrated

First published in 1981, this includes over 100 illustrations from the period 1901 to 1919 and is the second in the series of photographic records covering different periods. A second edition was published in 1990.

Croydon Between the Wars

First published in 1987, this includes over 100 illustrations from the period 1919 to 1939 and is the third in our photographic record series. A second edition was published in 1992.

Croydon in the 1940s and 1950s

Published in 1994, over 130 illustrations record the war years and the period leading up to the start of the massive redevelopment of the 1960s.

Croydon Old and New

First published in 1975, a completely new and enlarged fourth edition with 16 pages of colour illustrations was published in 1996.

Except for Croydon the story of a hundred years these publications can be obtained from local bookshops.
CNHSS has also published papers and reports on a variety of subjects of archaeological, historical and natural history interest. There is also a series of historical and modern postcards available.

Details of other publications will also be supplied on request (with SAE please), from

**The Secretary,
Croydon Natural History & Scientific Society,
96A Brighton Road, South Croydon, Surrey, CR2 6AD**